T0197395

Spring Into Love

A 21-Day Love Bloom

REINA ALEJANDRA PRADO

Balboa Press books may be ordered through booksellers or by contacting:

Balboa Press
A Division of Hay House
1663 Liberty Drive
Bloomington, IN 47403
www.balboapress.com
844-682-1282

Because of the dynamic nature of the Internet, any web addresses or links contained in this book may have changed since publication and may no longer be valid. The views expressed in this work are solely those of the author and do not necessarily reflect the views of the publisher, and the publisher hereby disclaims any responsibility for them.

Cover Image and Author Photo by: Elijah Richard

ISBN: 978-1-9822-7616-4 (sc)
ISBN: 978-1-9822-7617-1 (e)

Print information available on the last page.

Balboa Press rev. date: 11/10/2021

This book is dedicated to my clients, who allow me to witness their bloom and deepen their capacity to love themselves.

Spring Into Love is a 21-day program that I delivered daily via my newsletter. The intention was to invite folks to spring into love through a series of prompts and guided experiences where folks reflected on love and beliefs about relationships. The process helped them notice patterns that rooted in moments that caused a type of wounding. Also, it allowed them to remember to honor the love stories that they carried as it encouraged them to deepen their capacity to love.

The series was offered in March 2021 to help prepare one's heart to be in a different space by the time Spring Equinox arrived. Following the Mayan sacred calendar, participants tuned into the energy of the wanderer to open up their heart and engage with the process with curiosity. The guided experiences followed the energy of two trecenas (13 day cycles) that are Kej & Ajpu. The energy of Kej is known for its strength and vitality. How can we apply this our actions when it comes for Love? The subsequent trecena Ajpu is the invitation to plant the seed of what Love you want to bring into the world. The energies during these days inspired many of the reflection prompts and guided experiences. I decided not to change the content of the recordings, as this work emerged and was co-created in alignment with these energies. The audio link will take you to my sound cloud page where you can listen to the album *Spring Into Love*. You can access it via the cloud icon found on may page linktr.ee/healingqueen

You can begin the 21-day bloom when you are ready to expand your love vibration. I recommend starting on a new moon so that you follow the daily sequence throughout a moon cycle. I call it a "21-day bloom" because I have an aversion to the word "challenge" that circulates in many programs. **Spring Into Love** supports you to bloom at your pace while expanding your love vibration.

The daily prompts are structured with a set time limit. I know these will feel short. They are formatted this way so that you get into a space to freely write without censoring yourself. I ask that you jump in and write what comes through at the moment and not take time to think about the answer. Our mind or ego has a way to protect us and not do things that may seem hurtful. When prompts feel like too much and is awakening pain or discomfort in your body, take a breath and let the energy of the emotion have its cycle alongside the inhale and exhale of your breath. Folks can choose to focus solely on the written prompts or engage with the guided experience as each activity can stand on its own.

As you begin the 21-day experience, I invite you to consider the following agreements to make the most of your experience:

- You are a divine being of love.
- Love is your entitlement.

- Listen from the space of your heart / soul and not your ego-mind. When your ego wants to challenge or object, notice what awakened this response. Take a breath and explore what is showing up in the moment.
- Regardless of your lived experiences in past relationships, remember you are a perfect expression and creation of love.
- Everyone has their own story about love or love stories that have shaped their perceptions about love. When we base our love solely on these stories, we miss out on the expansive nature of love as a vibration not just an emotion.

The motivation behind this work stems from my own practice as a Love Conscious Coach who began offering Love Limpias, which are energetic clearings of the heart space, to clients who sought to connect to their most authentic self. I created workshops and group coaching programs to support an individual to understand with compassion their woundedness around Love. Through energy healing and ancestral teachings, I guide folks to understand the root causes of feeling disempowered or unloved. Clients then clear limiting beliefs around Love and invite a transformation to emerge, thereby becoming resourced as they reclaim their connection to Love as an expansive force in their lives.

I offer sessions in the Kizh / Gabrielino Tongva Territories in Southern California, and work remotely with clients and via the spaces Minka in Brooklyn, NY, Rainbow Soul Collective in Gloucester, MA, and Mostly Angels in Los Angeles, CA. What I share here is an evolution of my various love offerings that began over twenty years with the poem entitled "Santa Perversa" and an interactive performance piece that I named "Take a Piece of My Heart."

I added an appendix of self-care tips for our physical, emotional, mental, and spiritual bodies. You can source from these suggestions and others included throughout the text to support you on this 21-day journey. Another series of prompts to connect with the planetary energy of the days. I would love to hear about your experience with the series. Feel free to reach out and ask questions too. Best way to reach me is via my website www.healingqueen.org or Instagram page @healingqueen_

Wishing you continued blessings and expansion of your love vibration,

Reina Alejandra Prado
Love Conscious Coach and Holistic Energy Practitioner

*Lighten your heart so that it
may be as light as a feather.*

Day 1: *I Explore My Connection to Love*

The following prompts are to help you recognize any undercurrents that may create stagnation or attachments to an ideal of 'love' instead of being in the vibration of Love. Answer as many of the prompts you want. I recommend setting a timer for **5 minutes** to answer each prompt. You should spend no more than 20 minutes on this exercise. This way you can free-write with less of a filter and allow your truth to emerge uncensored.

Reflect on the following:

1. What in your life, space, or energy needs to be cleared and / or cleansed to make room for love?
2. When is your love energy in harmony and when do you perceive it not to be in harmony? First, connect to this feeling of harmony in your body. What quality or texture does it have? Where does it reside in your body? Use a memory when you experienced harmony to activate this somatic connection.
3. What areas in your life are most vibrant with the frequency of love and where in your life do you want to elevate the vibration more?
4. When are you most tender and loving with yourself, and when are you not?

Supplemental Activity:

Begin to create a space in your home where you drop in to do this work. The more consistency you create, the easier you mind can support you in your heart's journey. In this space place the tools that will support you, such as crystals or essential oils. Diffuse oils such as rose, geranium, or any other plant or flower ally that awakens the connection to your heart. Create a crystal grid with rose quartz, malachite, aventurine, labradorite, selenite, clear quartz, and/or amethyst. Trust your intuition on which crystals to use in your grid. A crystal grid is energetically arranging a group of crystals to follow a sacred geometric shape like the Seed of Life or the Flower of Life in order to support an intention and/or manifestation.

Day 2: *I Reflect on My Relationships*

The *Course in Miracles* teaches us that every relationship mirror backs something about ourselves. Often the ego will implement tools or ideas such as sacrifice, guilt, anger, or suffering to create demands from one another, particularly of those who have hurt us. If we can remember that "sacrifice is attack, not love," and that "[g]uilt cannot last when the idea of sacrifice has been removed;" then we can experience love and know peace is possible (pages 314-320).

To experience this love and peace can be challenging in the day to day, as there will be moments when the ones we love will inevitably hurt us. Dr. Gary Zukav elaborates more on this by sharing that often the tender parts of our heart are awakened when our spiritual partner can say or do something that reopens a wound to our broken heart.

Today, I invite you to take a moment to reflect on your relationships as it can offer some insight on what projections you may still have about yourself and the relationships you have experienced. Set the timer for 15 minutes to complete the prompt. If reflecting gets difficult, I invite you to practice a mindfulness technique of non-attachment I learned from Sharon Salzburg in their book *Real Love*:

- Recognize what is happening in the moment.
- Acknowledge your feelings occurring in the moment.
- Investigate the origin of these feelings or root of the wound.
- Imagine you are not attached to the energetic weight of the moment.
- Nurture your heart.

Reflect on the following:

1. Think of 3 moments when you experienced heartbreak. Notice that I wrote heartbreak as our hearts can experience hurt which feels like heart break even in non-intimate relationships.
2. As you select your top three, do not go into the energy of the pain even though your ego will want you to.
3. Instead, consider what you learned about your capacity to love in that moment? This will be a good exercise to practice non-attachment to the energy of those moments. If you are experiencing getting emotionally charged up, then there may be some unresolved energy.

Day 3: *I Am Love*

"I AM" are the most potent words, as they encapsulate the fullness of your soul's connection to your higher self. When we feel loved, secure, and at peace this is when our true self is able to radiate out this energy. When you can consciously connect to the vibration of **"I Am Love"**, then you have a greater capacity to experience these heart-to-heart connections. By affirming **"I Am Love"** we also invite our mind to believe it and not an older story(ies) of I am not loveable. By proclaiming the **"I Am"** you are calling on the divine energy of the Creator of all that is, God, Universe, and Spirit. However, you name it, remember you are a divine expression and reflection of this love.

Yesterday we unearthed the wisdom from past relationships, and I invited you to release the energetic weight of any of these moments that still weighed down your heart. You began to heal some tender areas of your spirit. If you are still processing what you experienced yesterday, continue to identify what you are noticing in your body and energy field today. Do not focus on what you felt when the heartbreak happened.

Today the invitation is to reflect on the light of love that you may have felt in relationships. Similar to yesterday's prompts I encourage you to do the following. This is another mindfulness teaching by Lama Rod Owens S.N.O.E.L.L. in *Love and Rage*, pages 61-65:

1. **See it** - When you can see/feel what the "it" is that you are working through, then your mind can process it.
2. **Name It** - Label the sensations you are experiencing
3. **Own It** - It's a process to help us accept what we are going through.
4. **Experience it** - Be in a space of neutrality to witness how the moment/memory is affecting you, whether positively or negatively.
5. **Let it Go** - Letting go means to make a choice to not carry the energetic weight of it in our heart.
6. **Let it Float** - Experience letting go and notice how the body, mind, or energy field has shifted after you have gone through this process.

Answer as many of the prompts you want. I recommend setting a timer for **20 minutes** to answer all the prompts. This way you free-write with less of a filter and allow your truh to emerge uncensored.

Reflect on the following:

1. Identify 3 moments when you felt most loved. This can include feeling cherished, secure, loved, worthy, like you belong, at peace, or understanding.
   a. If your truth feels like you've never been loved, then focus on moments when you practiced acts of self-love.
2. Based on these moments, how would you define the experience of love?
3. Are any of these experiences of love still applicable in your life today? Do you still see love in these ways? If not, then what has shifted your perspective?
4. In what ways do you model love and make others feel cherished, secure, love, worthy, like they belong, at peace, and understood?

Day 4: I Am an Agent of Love

Yesterday we proclaimed **I am Love**. How did it feel to do so? What did you notice? Does your heart feel a little lighter?

Today, we continue with this practice by learning to lighten our heart in our day-to-day experiences, thus becoming an agent of Love. When we live love as a reality, as a way of seeing the world, as a way of being in the world then we are better equipped to act in service of Love.

One of the ways to do this is to acknowledge in what ways we weigh our heart down. This can happen in habitual behaviors or in believing that we are only capable of love or worthy of love. The aim is, as Jennifer Sodini says, to "make the unconscious conscious [as] each ripple of purity expands into the collective, allowing for a more fluid evolution to flow forward with a feathered heart - connected to all but attached to no thing" (*Living with a Feathered Heart*, p110). Yes, it is published as "no thing," not "nothing."

Often, experiences and situations with people we love may have forced us to create these habits or beliefs as a means of protecting our heart from heartbreak. For example, "I only attract _____ and this is why I cannot be in healthy relationships." Or someone modeled for you that the only way to receive love is doing everything they ask, and love or affection becomes a reward not the expansive vibration that it is.

Answer as many of the prompts you want. I recommend setting a timer for **20 minutes** to answer all the prompts. This way you free-write with less of a filter and allow your truth to emerge uncensored. Go with your first thought and try not to over think them.

Reflect on the following:

1. Based on the wisdom obtained from heartbreaks and when you felt most loved, articulate what is your love story in 3 sentences or less. If you did not complete the prompts for days 2 & 3 then write your love story as you experience it today. It can begin with ... "My love story feels like I am ..."
2. Based on this love story, what expectations or conditions must be met for you to be loved? Write this out as a list. Take at most 3 minutes to do so.
3. Consider which of these expectations or conditions creates more weight in your heart.
4. Could you still be an agent of Love if this expectation or condition was met?

Day 5: *I Surrender to Love's Flow*

Surrender may be difficult to practice in our day-to-day activities. When we truly do surrender and relinquish any attachment to a set outcome then we can appreciate how Divine timing is always on-time, even though it may not be on our time. When a challenge manifests, we can lose our sense of peace and prefer to rely on our perception(s) of what should be and how it should show up. The *Course in Miracles* states "Judgment is the process on which perception but not knowledge rests….In the presence of knowledge all judgement is automatically suspended, and this is the process that enables recognition to replace perception" (pages 46-47). Knowledge stems from a truth informed by our higher self. In the recognition, we are in a state of presence and our heart can experience peace without judgement.

However, our ego is not able to operate in a state of surrender because it wants a say in the outcome of things, events, or relationships come. This urge can inadvertently raise the fear factor, perceiving that not knowing an outcome or having no control on said outcome can be a dangerous proposition. What we do not realize is that, when we are in this space of needing to know for sure what will happen, we take ourselves out of the present moment. Only in the present moment can love be felt in its divine unfolding.

When it comes to love, I often hear clients share their concern that they may never love again or that they fear having their heart broken. The *Course in Miracles* reminds that "Love will enter immediately into any mind that truly wants it, but it must want it truly. This means that it wants it without ambivalence, and this kind of wanting is wholly without the ego's 'drive to get' "(page 61). In a state of surrender, it is possible to have the most beautiful heart-to-heart connections and to open ourselves up to the infinite possibilities.

Answer as many of the prompts below as you want. I recommend setting a timer of **5 minutes** per prompt. This way you free-write with less of a filter and allow your truth to emerge uncensored. Try not to over think these prompts, and go with your first thought.

Reflect on the following:

1. When you think of the notion of surrender what are some thoughts that come to mind? Make a note of how many are coming from a place of judgment or a sense of peace.
2. How can you practice surrender in your day-to-day life?
3. When it comes to love, how have you experienced surrender?

Supplemental Activity

Create a ritual bath with rose petals (organic preferred. If don't have access to organic then use food grade rosewater), rosemary, honey, cinnamon sticks. Use these ingredients or create your own blend. Brew them together until the water boils. Let the pot cool a bit, then strain it. Add the brew to your bath. (If you do not have a bathtub, you can do it as a foot soak. Imagine the love you are calling in, and release what no longer serves you in the water. For added touch of luxury add almond or coconut milk.

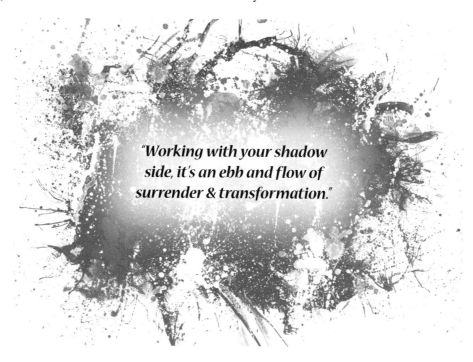

"Working with your shadow side, it's an ebb and flow of surrender & transformation."

Day 6: *I Transform Through Forgiveness*

You may be feeling a bit lost in your thoughts after this week's series of prompts. The invitation is to trust what has arisen and to allow the vibration of love to guide you. Take a moment to honor your willingness to spring into love more and more. When it comes to love, our thoughts can take up energetic space distracting us from one truth: Am I worthy of love? Have I done enough to earn it? Can I have it again? When will it come? **The truth is that you are Love.** It is already within you and there is no need to do anything to get it.

To help accept this truth, the *Course in Miracles* reminds us that "Forgiveness is the healing of the perception of separation" (page 46). When we believe that we are exiled from Love is when we forget our wholeness. To mend the perception of separation from Love and the love of others, we must practice atonement and forgiveness. The more one can practice this, the better we can experience the world through Love. The perception of separation is quelled.

The following prompts are inspired from Lesson 21 in the *Course in Miracles*. Complete each one and be aware that any prompt could reflect where you see the separation and what needs to shift to experience the forgiveness. Try to be as specific as possible. You can choose to write multiple entries for each prompt or write one situation for each one. It is up to you how you want to engage. Notice if any resistance arises as you write the prompt and meet with what is showing up with much compassion. Hold each thought until you notice the energy of the thought shift in your body. I recommend to write and experience the energy of each one before moving onto the other.

Do not over think these prompts and go with your first instinct. Set the timer for **15 minutes** and see how many you get done. You can always return to this prompt at any time during or after the 21 days.

1. I am determined to see _____ [name of person] differently.
2. I am determined to see _____ [specify the situation] differently.
3. I am determined to see _____ [specify the attribute] in _____ [name of person] differently.
4. I am determined to see myself in _____ [specify the situation] differently.
5. I am determined to see _____ specify the attribute} in myself differently.
6. Above all else I want to see this _____ differently.

Day 7: *I Am Open to All Forms of Love*

During our first week, you began to identify where and when barriers to Love may have arisen in your life. The invitation this week is to call in the love you want to experience by identifying preferred feelings when it comes to love. During the guided experiences, we will explore this connection through each of the chakras. When you have a clear sense of how you want to experience love, it will be easier to recognize it when it shows up. To be open to all forms of love is to understand that love is fluid and abundant.

Set the timer for **15 minutes** and see how many you get done. You will continue to explore this prompt today and tomorrow. These prompts are inspired by Danielle LaPorte's work.

1. Identify 3-5 preferred feelings in these areas: intimate relationship, family, and with yourself.
2. Identify which are your top 3 preferred feelings.
3. Once you are done identifying your preferred feelings, create an affirmative phrase or action statement with these words.
4. Another prompt to help you hone in on the preferred desired feelings is to write: *What is [insert here Preferred Feeling] really about for me?* This is great when using big words—and by big I mean words that have loaded meaning already. For example, words like love, peace, joy, confidence, beauty are a few that can be explored in depth.
5. You will continue working with your preferred feelings during the next few days until you hone in on those that reflect what you are ready to embody for yourself in terms of love.

Day 8: *I Claim the Love I Want*

Yesterday, you were invited to articulate the preferred feelings you want to experience when it comes to love. During the guided experience we began to work with your chakras to help clear out any energetic blocks that may exist. This week, we'll explore more about the love you are ready to call in. We'll do so by focusing on each energy center and incorporating the elements as well.

Sometimes the need to be right gets in the way of being freer in your capacity to be in the flow of love. This is because the ego prefers to be in the right. We can all think of a moment when in the midst of a discussion with a partner, lover, or friend our mind started to figure out ways to get the point across while not listening and being present. Ram Dass has shared that when being right is the aim, we can neither experience love nor be free.

As you formalize your words/phrases that exemplify your preferred feelings around love, tune into the energy of what arises in your body and your field when you say them out loud. Remember, you are staking a claim on the love that you want.

Set the timer for **15 minutes** and continue to finesse your list of core desired feelings.

1. Identify your top 3 preferred feelings about love. Refer to the list you created yesterday.
2. Use this prompt to help you clarify more your preferred feelings. *What is [insert here Preferred Feeling] really about for me?* If you still have words like love, peace, joy, confidence, beauty keep exploring what those feelings are about for you.
3. Once you are done identifying your preferred feelings then create an affirmative phrase or action statement with these words.

When you finish writing, keep it somewhere where you can meditate and continue refining your list this week.

Day 9: *I Create Healthy and Loving Relationships*

I invite you to finalize the list of preferred feelings you want to experience when it comes to love. As you formalize the words/phrases that exemplify your core desired feelings, tune into the energy of what arises in your body and in your field when you say them out loud. Remember, you are staking a claim on the love that you want.

This week, we explore more about the love you are ready to call in. We'll do so by focusing on each energy center, incorporating the elements, and amplifying the vibration of the core desired feelings in the guided experiences.

Let's face the elephant in the room, so to speak, and identify any undercurrents that may be operating in our subconscious mind. Am I worthy of being in a loving and healthy relationship? Given my experience in past relationships, can I ever experience love again? Let's begin with a belief that you are Love and, as such, are worthy of a love that is healthy, present, and expansive. Your past experiences do not define your capacity to love again. However, your mind/ego will have you believing that is the case. bell hooks writes in *Wounds of Passion, "I know that there is a way to love that frees. I know that there is a way to love that gives life. I know this even though I have not witnessed such love."* Even though you may or may not have experienced a healthy and loving relationship know that you are entitled to this kind of love.

How we demonstrate love and receive love is another aspect of creating healthy and loving relationships. The work of Dr. Gary Chapman on the five primary Love Languages began to open up this conversation in the mainstream. According to him, the top five love languages are: words of affirmation, quality time, physical touch, acts of service, and physical touch. When I teach the Love Languages in my workshop **Activating Divine Love**, I ask participants to identify their top two love languages so they can notice how they communicate their love languages and if they shift their love languages based on who the recipient of their love is.

The prompts today invite you to reflect a bit more on what is a loving and healthy relationship for you. When you can create an energetic shift on what you believe relationships should be like and begin to see them as co-creative partnerships, then love can feel more expansive, equitable, and freeing.

Set the timer for **20-minutes** total time. Try to answer each prompt in **5 minutes** or less. Do not edit your answers as you are writing.

1. Create two columns. On one side write what Love is and the other what Love is not. Create a list of 5-10 items.
2. From the list of What Love Is, which one feels most aligned with your Preferred Feelings on Love? If none feel aligned, then create a new list of What Love Is with your Preferred Feelings in mind.
3. Based on the idea of Love Languages by Dr. Gary Chapman, what are your two preferred ways to receive love? Do you also offer love in these ways? If you don't, when or why does it change?

Day 10: *I Am Rooted in Love*

If you have not done so yet, please finalize your preferred feelings and create your statement with them. Tune into the energy of what arises in your body and your field when saying them out loud. Remember, you are staking a claim on the love that you want.

Today we explore more about the love you are ready to call in by connecting to our root chakra and ancestors. The prompts are to inspire you to create the physical space for Love to be more centered and grounded in your day-to-day.

Answer each prompt with your first thought and do not edit your answers as you are writing. Set the timer for **20 minutes**.

1. Is Love something you think of as a reward, something to earn, or be worthy to receive?
    a. If you answered yes, what moment(s) rooted this belief as a truth in your being? Focus on this prompt to uncover an undercurrent that may be a block to your idea of love.
    b. If you answered no, then move on to the next prompt.
2. Whether you are in a relationship or not, how do you share your time with others from a space of Love instead of obligation? If you share from a space of obligation what can you shift so that it comes from Love instead?
3. For those of you seeking to meet your divine match, does your home/life have room for another person to be in it? For those of you in a relationship, how can you make room for your partner and you to reflect your growth as divinely matched beings?

I call upon the condor and the eagle to help me soar above my worries.
I call upon the hummingbird to remind me to be joyful in love.

Day 11: *I see myself as Love*

Today, we tune in to our vision and perception about love by tapping into our third-eye's view. Perception creates the separation of self from Spirit. When we see ourselves as part of Spirit, it is easier to connect to our Vision as being part of a whole. An analogy I have heard and shared is that you are not just a drop in the ocean, you are the ocean. Perception will have us believing that a drop cannot make any difference at all. In fact, a drop can create a ripple effect that we may or may witness its impact in our lifetime.

On the Mayan sacred calendar, the energy of Iq' invites us to be inspired by the divine and allow the words to flow from the space of your inner knowing. The animal associated with Iq' is that of the hummingbird. The hummingbird represents adaptability, versatility, and most importantly the inclination to pursue the sweetness of life from a place of joy.

Today's prompts and guided experience were inspired by the energy of the day 3 Iq. Given that we are on day 11th of our journey we are also entering a portal of personal change. This is your invitation to call in what you seek in Love.

Answer each prompt with your first thought and do not edit your answers as you are writing. Set the timer for **10 minutes** to complete each prompt. Notice that you are only to complete prompts 3 or 4 depending on what is your intention today.

1. What is the kind of love you want to experience more in your life? Answer for entry below.
   a. Yourself
   b. Your intimate partner / spouse
   c. Your family
2. Imagine your future self writes you a letter composed of wisdom, insight, rituals, and practices for love that you can implement from this point forward.
3. If you are ready to call in your divine match, use this prompt to start identifying what you seek in your partner/future spouse.
4. If you are already in a relationship, then use this prompt to identify how you want your relationship to feel more like a spiritual partnership.

Day 12: *I Speak Love into Existence*

I share a passage from Lama Rod Owens' book *Love and Rage: The Path of Liberation Through Anger,* "you also have an ethical responsibility to have a relationship with your hurt. I can be hurt and angry at the same time, and I can love both my anger and hurt." Owens reminds us how to be in relationship with our hurt. Often we prefer to bypass the hurt and communicate that "I'm okay" or "I'm good." In doing so, it's like we're swallowing our own truth and not speaking to the hurt or unloving act in the moment.

In the work of Polarity, the throat chakra is connected to the element ether. As ether, this energy center is not just about communication, it is also about listening, grieving and giving space to things so that a sense of freedom can emerge. Consider the following: How do we speak Love into existence? How do we express it from a place of our highest self and truth and not from a place of anxiousness or fear? How do we grieve and honor the emotions coming up instead of letting them fester in the pit our stomach or liver? I'm sure all of us can think of a moment when something like this happened and the sensation might have felt like a lump in our throat.

Today, embrace the clarity of mind that came from yesterday's prompts. It prepared you to step into your light and speak into existence your dreams of love and/or a loving relationship. Know that you have the support of the four directions to make this so.

For today's journaling, we are doing something different. There is no guided experience for this day. Instead, use yesterday's prompts to energize your voice to claim what you are ready to welcome as Love in your life.

1. Yesterday you wrote about the love you are ready to call in and/or the divine relationship or spiritual partnership you desire.
2. Today, give yourself permission to state your desire out loud to the four directions. If not ready to do this, then state out loud the following statements:
   a. Even though I have experienced heartbreaks, I am open to love with an open heart.
   b. Even though I am weary to trust that I can love again, I know I am a reflection of Divine Love.
   c. Even though I will be vulnerable opening myself to love again, I know I can trust my heart.
3. Reflect on how does your heart feels when you speak to that which you are ready to call in. If you stated the phrases, notice any shifts in your body and/or field.

Day 13: *I Co-Create with the Universe*

For the past week, you focused on the preferred feelings you want to experience and embody when it comes to love. You also spoke it out loud to the ether. The invitation today is to co-create with the Universe. There are no writing prompts for today; instead, do the guided experience and see what messages you receive from Universe, your guides, and/or your higher self. Write them down so you can revisit those messages in the future. If it inspires writing them as an affirmation, then do so. See example below:

I co-create with the Universe.
Rooted in my knowing
Aligning with my greatest and highest good & greatest joy.

Day 14: *My Love is Expansive*

These past two weeks, we have been tending to our beliefs around Love, and co-creating with the Universe a love that honors our Higher Self. Remember that Love grows with Love. That is today's theme for the prompts and guided experience.

Our human existence craves and seeks connection. After collectively navigating a global pandemic many of us are ready to be in the world again. When it comes to love, we know it when we experience it. This reminds me of the Whitney Houston song "How will I know if he really loves me?" Our mind / ego wants to know. It seeks certainty. In the craving of connection, we inadvertently create attachments to ideals, expectations, or beliefs around Love that inevitably lead to disappointment and heartbreak.

For today's prompts, the invitation is to think of the many ways you can be more expansive in your love. Because, when we are touched by love it leaves an imprint in our heart-soul space. Imagine when our love is expansive, it too can touch and connect to others in a similar way.

To help us in this process we are going to work on the final chakra of this week: the heart. I understand our heart chakra as actually having two centers of energy. One is located at the center of our chest, while the other is located just below the collarbone and by our thymus (higher heart chakra). In yesterday's guided experience, we started to connect to our higher heart chakra. This chakra is tied to our ability for selfless love.

For today's prompts set the timer for **20 minutes** and try to answer as many of the questions as you can. If you do not finish in **20 minutes**, notice which prompt you are overthinking. This may be where the energy is directing your focus.

1. How can you expand more your awareness around love to see, experience, and live its possibilities?
2. Where in your life do you perceive disconnects or fissures in your connection to love? Create a quick list of no more than 10.
3. Select one from the list and create an action plan of how you want to tend to this area by expanding it from a place of love. Try to start each step with a verb.
4. What is one actionable thing you can do today to set this in motion?
5. Track this week what you notice when you intentionally come from a place of love.

Day 15: *Love Deepens My Connections to Others*

When we love ourselves first, it deepens our connections and ability to love others. There is an analogy that I heard Sharon Salzburg once share in a meditation course. At one point in their life, they believed that Love was like something delivered by the UPS service: something that was brought to you from an external source. Then they would worry that if the Love was delivered to the wrong address it would be taken away that easily.

Often social and cultural cues have us believing that Love is a source outside of us that can be taken, or is only available to us if we're good and deserving of it. Another pattern that can manifest when we do not see Love as a source within us is that we lose ourselves in another, particularly in an intimate relationship. This can cause stress and feelings of anxiety, or can create self-destructive behaviors because we perceive love being unattainable and something outside of us.

However, the more you are able to experience inner peace and love with your true self, the easier it is to relate to others in this manner as well. When you listen with your body or create those somatic connections of what peace and love feel like, look like, or sound like in your body and your field, it becomes easier to notice what Love is and what it is not. It becomes easier to live your life according to your Love Wisdom.

When we began our journey, I invited you to contemplate areas in your life that are most vibrant with the frequency of love and where in your life do you want to elevate the vibration more? For today's prompts set the timer for **15 minutes** and free-write: how would you answer this question differently today versus when you first started this series? I also invite you this week to continue tracking the shifts in how your love expands. See yesterday's prompts.

Day 16: *I Am Attuned to Love*

Too often we may have wanted to listen to our heart's whispers of love, but our mind shushes those whispers, ignores our gut instinct, and squelches the butterflies in our stomach. We stop ourselves so as not to love too much, dream so big, or even be too much. What if we listened to those whispers and chose to live a life centered on love? By "a life centered on love," I do not just mean the emotion of it. I mean the expansive frequency of Love. Our lives and relationships become so much richer that we will not want to deprave ourselves of Love ever again.

The following acknowledgements can serve as a guide for ones that you will write for yourselves in your own words. These acknowledgements will serve as reminders in those moments when you cannot see yourself as Love. Identify a moment that has prevented or made you not act on the love you felt or sought. Follow it up with a statement on how you will still be able to love.

- I acknowledge that I may experience heartbreak again. That will not stop me from experiencing love.
- I acknowledge that the tender wounds of being unloved will arise when I perceive or experience being unloved again.
- I acknowledge that folks will come in and out of my life like seasons. Some may be there for a shorter period while others may be a lifetime. I will love them fully when they are here. I will remember them lovingly when they are not.
- I acknowledge that my capacity to love is not defined by how others are able to love me in return.

There is no guided experience for the next three days. For the next three days, I invite you to practice Louise Hayes' Mirror Work. Do the Mirror Work every day at the same time?

When I have done this work it has had a deep impact on healing my wounds of feeling unloved. To this day, I still cry when I do partner work at a workshop and listen to a stranger share what they love about me and I reciprocate. It affirms that love can be felt and reciprocated even with strangers.

On the first day, set the timer for **10 minutes**. If that feels too long, then start at 5 minutes and build up to 10 minutes by the third day. If starting at 10 minutes build up to 20 minutes by the time you get to day three. Sit in front of a mirror and begin to state out loud "I Love You" a few times. Yes, this will feel awkward and possibly silly. Then continue to state out loud self-loving positive affirmations, or state what you love about yourself. Notice when the voice of judgement or critique rises. Also, where in your body something softens or tightens. Afterwards, free-write about this experience. Review what you wrote until after the third day. What patterns showed up for you? In what ways were you able to be more loving to yourself and others when you did the mirror work? What surprised you?

Love is the vibrational exponential force that reverberates through our hearts.

Day 17: *My Love Fills the Room*

How often are you told that your smile lights up a room? Or, that your energy is larger than life? Do you hear these statements as compliments or do you tend to make yourself smaller? In our desire to be loved, we inadvertently make our energy, presence, or love smaller because _____ (fill in the blank). Alex Elle shares a beautiful reminder to not shrink ourselves to "fit into the hearts of people who aren't able to love" us in the ways we deserve to be loved. I would add that we also not shrink our love and only make it available under certain conditions.

The process of making ourselves smaller happens at a young age in an unconscious manner. There is a moment when the choice to mold yourself in ways that you perceive will make you be more loved by certain folks in your life, i.e. parents, siblings, aunties, uncles, grandparents, friends, has you doing things that compromise a sense of your true self. Also, at a young age, you mirror the love you see expressed in the home, family, and community. The molding, or making yourself different to be loved or liked by others, may facilitate the shrinkage of your true self. At some point, you choose to stop behaving in these ways. You act different or indifferent to receive their love. Yet, somewhere inside there is still a yearning.

Here is the crux of the matter: How do we tend to the yearning of the heart while not shrinking to fit into other hearts? We meet the roots of the yearning with compassion and invite that energy to transform into a bloom of self-love. This is where the practice of expanding your love vibration enables you to detach from the quest of getting love. The more you practice the easier it becomes to see yourself as Love: a love that fills the room and beyond.

For today's writing prompt, I invite you to set the timer for **20-30 minutes**. Read through the questions first. Answer as many as you can. If you cannot write it out, record an audio memo and talk it out. If you do not finish when the timer goes off, then honor what came through in the moment. There is still medicine there.

1. Free write about a moment or memory when you shrank your heart or your true self.
2. How is that moment / memory still impacting your choices today when you shrink your heart or true self?
3. What is an actionable step you can take today to be more expansive in your love vibration and that will not allow you to shrink your heart anymore?

Day 18: *I Listen with My Heart*

You are days away from completing the 21-day bloom. Please know that you can connect to *Spring Into Love* at any time. I suggest that when you do, to come from a place of who you are in the moment and not who you were when you first went through this 21-day bloom. This will allow for new insight.

Today, the invitation is to listen with your heart in order to be of greater service to yourself, your loved ones, and your community. When we lead our lives from a heart-centered place, we are much more capable of being compassionate, understanding, and patient with ourselves and others. A heart centered life does not operate separate from the mind; it is in relationship to it. Our mind would have us believe that a heart-led life is dangerous and frivolous.

This reminds me of the cartoon *"Inner Workings"* (2016) by Leo Matsuda that screened before *Moana*. We follow a young man as he is getting ready to go to work. The mind stops any action that could be distracting, indulgent, or fun, seeing them all as dangerous. The mind eventually realizes that the heart has atrophied and allows it to take the lead at the end of the cartoon. When the heart takes over, the man enjoys his life, finds love, and inspires others to do the same.

Similarly, when we have experienced difficult moments, our mind lovingly protects us from going through it again. It's like, why do you want to experience hurt again? However, in doing this over and over, it can create thoughts and habits that may have us miss what makes our heart more open. This is when the listening becomes key in our well-being.

In a few of the guided experiences, I invited you to listen to your soul's and heart's wisdom. Continue to do so and notice if life feels more resonant with your true self. When you follow this wisdom and not your mind's how do you show up in the world differently? Do folks respond to you differently?

There is no writing prompt for today. Instead use the time to review what you wrote in the past three days from doing the *Mirror Work* by Louis Hayes. What patterns showed up? What shifted? What softened?

Day 19: *I Radiate Love*

We're now in the home stretch of this 21-day bloom.

Through these past three weeks you have increased your love vibration even more. When one radiates more love, it is easier to recognize when illusions or perceptions derail us from being in this highest vibration. They will show up again in moments when we get in an argument with our spouse, intimate partner, family member, or close friend. Our ego will have us believing that the separation between us is far greater, whereas love will remind us that there is no separation.

The Course in Miracles states that we can pass illusions, "as we seek to reach to what is true in us, and feel its all-embracing tenderness, its Love which us perfect as itself, its sight which is the gift, its Love bestows on us. We learn the way today." So today's practice comes from Lesson 28 in *The Course in Miracle*: It invites us to see things differently. When we do this from a place of Love, "you will see all things differently" in many situations and your relationships. As you do this practice more and more, one will understand more clearly what undercurrent(s) is(are) being driven by the energy of fear and not love.

For today's prompts set the timer for **15 minutes**. Create a list of things, situations, and/or relationships you want to see differently starting today. Though you will not get resolution on them today, the premise is that you are identifying dynamics that you are ready to see differently through the lens of Love and not Fear. I recommend creating a list of 5-10. If you want to switch out "see" for "Love" on some of these, you can do so as well.

Above all else I want to see＿＿＿＿＿＿＿＿＿＿＿ differently.

or

Above all else I want to love ＿＿＿＿＿＿＿＿＿＿＿ differently.

Once you create your list of 5-10, then select one to work on. Create a small actionable item to help you see/love differently that one thing on your list.

Day 20: *I Am a Magnet for Love*

There is a way that the earth shows us how to be a magnet for Love. Consider that the Earth magnetizes all that it loves in unconditional ways — always providing for our well-being through the food we eat and air we breathe, etc. We could not pull away even if we wanted to. Similarly, the frequency of Love operates in this way too. It is always there waiting for us to connect again. It does not leave us because we stop being loving or return to our stubborn habits, the frequency of Love does not diminish.

I am also reminded of the crystal Hematite. It was once known as the "Iron Rose" because of the properties of iron and metal that created a red tinge in the grey/black luster of the stone. Hematite is a grounding stone and also helps stop limiting beliefs or unhealthy emotions to arise. It is also a magnet. I admire Hematite's qualities because it serves as a reminder of how to be a solid magnet for Love: be grounded in who you are at your core. When you have clarity on your values and what you seek in a divine partner or what you want to cultivate in a divine relationship it is harder to waiver from your True Self. You will act accordingly.

Here is a new thought: *As I radiate Love, I am also a magnet for Love.*

For today's prompts, the invitation is to contemplate the ways you can be more grounded in your values as to attract complimentary energies that magnetize and amplify your Love frequency. As you go through the prompts try not to self-judge your answers. Though you are blooming more in Love, there will be moments where your default mode is what you know. We are creating practices that help you catch yourself and shift the energy towards love.

Set the timer for **20 minutes**.

- What are the values that reflect your true self?
- Of these values, how do you want your relationships to match and/or complement you?
- Identify one way that you start this today.

Day 21: *I Tend to My Love Garden*

Congratulations on making it to day 21 of our Spring Into Love offering. We are now in a new season. I invite you to keep watering those dream seeds of Love throughout this season. Shine your light. Continue to nurture and expand your Love vibration. Throughout these past 21 days, you have learned some new ways to do so. By creating small actionable steps daily, your love frequency amplifies.

For your final writing prompt, I invite you to write what is the **Love-Wisdom** you want to live by this season, this year, this lifetime?

- Set the timer for 5 minutes and free-write.
- Set the timer again for 5 minutes to go through what you wrote and highlight keywords or phrases that feel resonant with your higher self.
- For the next 5 minutes write your Love-Wisdom statement using the keywords and phrases you highlighted.
- Take another 5 minutes to see how aligned they are with your core desired feelings. Remember those from week 2? The core desired feelings will help affirm and/or reflect that you are abiding by your Love-Wisdom. Adjust as needed.

When the preferred feelings about Love and your Love-Wisdom become embodied experiences, it'll be easier to sense, feel, know when you are not in alignment with your true self.

Bonus Prompt: Reflect on how much you have grown since you began the series.

Supplemental Guide to Self-Love Practices

I invite you to expand upon the guide with your knowledge and experience. So much of my motivation to share this work is so that we may live a more **joyful, heart-led life**. When you ponder what that would look like/feel like for you, think: what do you notice waking up in your body and energy field? These **somatic cues** remind you of a knowing that is within you to guide you on how to make this a reality.

First, we must begin by dismantling the belief that one can only experience joy, love, and self-love or self-care solely as a reward. *Read that sentence again.* These practices are not rewards, yet we act on them as if they are. Remember that you are a divine being of love and a perfect creation. When we begin from this premise instead of the reward, we remember that **we are entitled to experience more joy and love**. However, we often have too much in our emotional closets to allow ourselves to live from our divinity.

Create a list of 5-10 things that you do already to support self-love and self-care practices. On that list, identify which ones you do daily, weekly, monthly, seasonally, or yearly. How many of these do you only do as a reward or when you have time? The shift from doing to being is that you engage them as a lifestyle instead of a special treat.

Our **emotional closets** are the areas of our thinking that may create habits, beliefs, and behaviors that often block our ability to live a joyful, heart-led life. These may come up around our thoughts about love, worthiness, trust. We may believe we do not have enough resources to experience self-love through various types of self-care practices fully. Sign up any workshop series **Love You** and **The Hummingbird's Map**. To learn how to live a more joyful, heart-led life, sign up for group coaching programs **Alchemy of True Self** or **Ámate** via my website www.healingqueen.abmp.com or linktr.ee/healingqueen

Another thing to remember is that our self-love or self-care practices impact all **our bodies and energy fields**. We tend to only think of its impact on our physical body. However, it will impact positively our mental, emotional, and spiritual bodies as well. When we intentionally create a life where we center joy and love, we can feel the ripple in our daily interactions.

The following pages are a suggested list of self-love practices that can support your physical, mental, emotional, and spiritual well-being. Remember, these practices do not require a substantial financial investment. Yet, they do require a commitment on your part to activate the divine love within so that you live in greater alignment with your heart and higher self.

Guide of Self-Love Practices

Select any from this list any that resonate with you. Then, add the ones you listed earlier to the different bodies it will support. Be mindful of which ones you want to daily, weekly, monthly, seasonally, or yearly. Notice when aspects of your emotional closet start to appear as part of that old thought that self-love practices are only a reward.

Body

Rest – This is more than just getting the suggested 6-8 hours of sleep. Make sure your sleep is restful. When the parasympathetic system can come to a state of relaxation, it helps the body to regenerate. Even our seven chakra centers do their own self-cleaning while we sleep.

Food – What foods elevate your energy and vibration, and which ones diminish it? It is not about depriving yourself of your favorite foods but rather making more energetic choices and not creating "cheat" moments. If you are going to indulge, then enjoy it fully. Bonus: eat foods that help balance the elemental energies in your body – fire, water, earth, and air. To learn more about this, sign up for my workshop All is Elemental.

Exercise – This is more than just going to the gym or doing some form of body-engaged activity. How are you getting more movement in your body? How are you spending time outdoors?

Baños (Baths) – Creating herbal baths with Epsom salt can help relax the body and mind. Doing these around moon cycles like the new moon or full moon adds another experience to your self-love and self-care practices.

Working with the elements – Deepen a connection with Earth, Water, Air, and Fire. The fire is being in the sun or doing a ritual with fire either with a candle or bonfire. For the earth, work in the garden and/or commune with your house plants. With water, I shared about the baños. You can also do this while washing your hands with an enchantment of what you want to amplify and release. Finally, for the air element let the wind kiss your body and dance with the wind as you gently sway your body.

Mental

Unplug – How often do you unplug from your devices, including the television, radio, and computer? The electromagnetic field (EMF) we experience from all electronic devices impacts our bodies. Crystals such as noble shungite, lepidolite, aventurine, fluorite, or black tourmaline are good to have around your devices to help diminish the impact of EMF.

Curiosity – How do you keep your curiosity and desire to learn growing? Make time to read, listen to a podcast, or sign up for a class to learn something new about yourself and/or deepen your knowledge in any area that is already familiar.

Creativity – We are all creative beings. Take some time to play creatively without investment in a fixed outcome, such as making something to sell or perfect. You can also do dance, singing, drawing, painting, collage, playing an instrument, or DJing. (This last one is my favorite one to do).

Release Perfectionism – Perfectionism is something we all have put on ourselves as a measure of our capacity to be good or worthy. Focus more on your integrity.

Meditation – Studies have found that meditation helps to quiet the mind. Listen to my guided meditations/experiences on my sound cloud page.

Emotional

Be with your feelings – Oftentimes, we do not give our emotions the attention they need. Our emotions offer us cues about what may be off-balance in our body and/or field. Like the breath that ebbs and flows, we can allow the energy of our feelings circulate. When we connect to what awakens the emotion(s), then we have an opportunity to **R.A.I.N., a mindful practice** from Sharon Salzburg's book Real Love.

- Recognize – what is happening at the moment
- Acknowledge – the feeling(s)/emotion(s) that arise.
- Investigate – when did these emotions take root?

- Non-Attachment / Nurture – release the energetic weight of the emotional origins and nurture yourself.

Shadow Work – This is not something that is done once in a session. It is the practice. We need to do the shadow work to notice the edges of our light and areas where growth and transformation can happen. If you are ready to explore this more within yourself, book a private coaching or Love Limpia session with me.

Morning Pages – This is such a great practice by Julia Cameron, published in *The Artist's Way*. Morning pages can help us create emotional distance from what may be preoccupying our minds. Morning pages can also help our mental body as we channel what's weighing on our minds to put it on paper.

Mirror Work – Louise Hay offered this practice of telling ourselves positive affirmations for 21 continuous days. It's hard to do at first because often, the negative self-talk and criticism come out first. But, the more you practice, the more your mind begins to shift and choose first the positive affirmation.

Mantras & Affirmations – The use of a repetitive phrase such as a mantra helps your mental and emotional bodies connect to the words' vibration. Affirmations work similarly in a way that the mind supports the emotional body, thereby amplifying the vibration.

Spiritual

Cleanse & clear your energy – Create a regimen to cleanse and clear your energy. Do this by burning sacred smokes, using cold water in the shower, using a selenite wand to wave over your body as an energetic wash, and/or clearing your energy field.

Spirit Guides/Angels – Create time to communicate with your Spirit Guides and Angels. As you deepen this practice by speaking with your guides, angels, and benevolent ancestors, create a language key to identify them.

Ancestors – Cultivate a connection with your benevolent ancestors. Create an altar to them and make offerings.

Personal Rituals – Personal rituals can include but are not limited to: pulling tarot cards, oracle cards, runes, or using other divination tools that can help you awaken your gifts of channeling.

Rising with the Sun – Welcoming the morning light can be a beautiful ground-in practice. You can create a ritual honoring the 7 directions. Sing to the sun and birds. Do sun-salutations.

Plant Medicine – Using flower essences, essential oils, or herbs can be helpful to create practices of self-love and self-care to support all four bodies. Be sure to do your research and learn of any contra-indications.

Crystals – Similar to plant medicine, crystals are another resource to support your four bodies as well. You can always look up the metaphysical properties of crystals and plants to support your well-being. Remember, we are co-creating with vibration. Your body is the most significant alchemical force!

Timing your self-love and self-care practices

Find your flow of what supports your well-being at any given moment. Trust it. Much of what I share here, I do myself. I hope this list helps you find your way to honor the fullness of you so that you may live a joyful heart-led life. I'm here to support you on your journey.

Self-Love prompts to align with the energy of the days

These prompts on Love are to help connect you to the planetary energy of the days. It was originally shared on my Instagram page. I find that co-creating with the energy of the days can help focus my attention and energy with the task at hand. I began with Mercury and ended with Mars. You can start any day of the week and follow the sequence for the seven days. Notice what comes up for you.

On this day of Mercury consider: How do you communicate how you want to be loved?

This is beyond the concept of love languages. Take a moment to think about how do you model, share, speak to the ways you want to be loved? Sometimes, we get this idea that folks should know how to love us. Remember no one is a mind reader. even if they are intuitive it does not mean they know how YOU want to be loved. The invitation today is to speak the ways you want to be loved. Share this in all your relationships, including spouses, partners, lovers, friends, family, etc.

On this day of Jupiter consider: How big is your love?

You're invited to have your love energy be expansive, big, generous, and benevolent like the planet Jupiter, not to act as if it'll be taken from us. At some point, you may have experienced it being given conditionally.

Love is not conditional. Love is open. Love is not something you trade to prove you're worthy of it. Love is Love. Love loves you unconditionally. Its vibration wants to open your heart more.

On this day of Venus consider: Why are you searching for Love?

Today, we are reminded that we don't need to search for Love when we remember we are Love.

Remember each one of us are this luminous field. Start acting as such.

On this day of Saturn consider: Relationships are not work. They're an invitation to be mindfully loving.

We deem the planet Saturn as the task master. What if we understand Saturn as the planet that helps us create safe containers to practice discipline in order to support becoming our best selves. In so doing, Saturn will feel less like it's testing our faith even when things aren't going our way. When you know thyself you will behave accordingly.

So what does this have to do with relationships? Everything. Saturn will have us believe that all we do requires work and it's a chore. When we come from a place and energy of love then it's not work. It's a practice. We remember our joy.

Today, I invite you to welcome a new thought that relationships are not work. They're an invitation to be mindfully loving to one another. When you practice being in relationships, your capacity for compassion and patience expands. You become more understanding. The critical voice & la queja (the complaint) diminishes Love exponentially.

On this day of the Sun consider: Does your love radiate as bright as the Sun?

On this day that we honor the Sun, I invite you to reflect; does your love radiate as bright as the Sun? Or, do you dim/magnify your love based on who sees it? Do you withdraw your love because you perceive it is not being reciprocated? The Sun does not dim, magnify, or withdraw its radiance. It shines for all because it is the Sun. You too are luminous like the Sun. I invite you to explore ways your love can radiate more each today. As you implement this practice for yourself others will gravitate to your warmth and loving radiance.

On this day of the Moon consider: You are whole like the moon.

The moon is always whole we just see it in phases. Often, my clients feel something is incomplete when in the area of love is not where they hope it'll be. This thought emerges when you believe you're separate from the vibration of Love. When we remember we are Love then there is no lack or thought that we're incomplete in our life. In those moments, when you're not felling as full with Love then I invite you to think of them as phases of Love.

The following prompts use the phases of the moon to see how your love goes through phases:

- How do you connect with vibration of Love?
- How do you stimulate this connection to Love?
- How do you notice when your love grows?
- How do you resource your love?
- How do you celebrate Love?
- How do you share your love?
- When does your love diminish?
- How do you restore your connection to Love?

On this day of the Mars consider: Love takes a stand.

Today, I invite you to embrace your divine masculine energy. We often associate Mars as the God of War. What if today's energy is more about the focus, drive and discipline to go for what's yours already. We do not tend to think of Love's energy as being this driven. Love does not waiver. It takes a stand for what is Love. Where do you take a stand for Love in your life? When do you honor your integrity and when do you compromise it?

I share an excerpt of a channeled message from Ascended Master Guinevere that speaks to this:

"Love is a luminous field of potentiality. You get caught in the fixity of outcomes that you can't see all the love makes possible. .... Love is not a burden. It's a gift. A gift that is precious. Treat it as such."

ABOUT THE AUTHOR

Reina Prado is a bi-lingual Love Conscious Coach and Holistic Energy Practitioner who co-creates with folks ready to experience a more dynamic connection to Love. They offer workshops and group coaching programs to support participants reclaim their joy and live a heart-led life, such as in *The Hummingbird's Map, Love You* Series, *Ámate*, and *Alchemy of True Self*. Check out their podcast *Activating Divine Love* and recorded guided experiences on their Sound Cloud and YouTube pages. Their signature offering Love Limpias, which are energetic clearings of the heart space, can be experienced virtually and in-person in the Los Angeles area. Follow them on Instagram @healingqueen_. For more information about their services and programs, head to their sites: www.healingqueen.org and https://linktr.ee/healingqueen.

Printed in the United States
by Baker & Taylor Publisher Services